North

BRITISH COLUMBIA
Canada

Vancouver

Salish Sea

WASHINGTON
United States

Puget Sound

Seattle

Manchester

Vashon
Island

For Springer's team and fellow dreamers — D.S.

For Luella and Jonah — S.B.

Acknowledgments

Deepest thanks to John Ford, Erich Hoyt, Joe Scordino, Lynne Barre, Pete Schroeder, Ellen Drury, Kathy Fletcher, Ken Weiner and Lisa Hiruki-Raring for reviewing the manuscript. Special thanks to Anne Jackson of the 'Namgis First Nation for providing cultural guidance and expertise.

The sign that appears on page 84 is an illustration of a carving by artist Blackie Dick. Thank you to his family for giving permission for this illustration to be included and to the Village of Alert Bay and U'mista Cultural Center for assistance.

Published in Canada and the U.S. by Kids Can Press Ltd.
25 Dockside Drive, Toronto, ON M5A 0B5

Kids Can Press is a Corus Entertainment Inc. company

www.kidscanpress.com

The artwork in this book was rendered in watercolor.
The text is set in Avenir.

Edited by Kathleen Keenan
Designed by Andrew Dupuis

Printed and bound in Dongguan, Guangdong, P.R. China, in 3/2021 by Toppan Leefung

CM 21 0 9 8 7 6 5 4 3 2 1

Library and Archives Canada Cataloguing in Publication

Title: Orca rescue! : the true story of an orphaned orca named Springer / written by Donna Sandstrom ; illustrated by Sarah Burwash.
Names: Sandstrom, Donna, author. | Burwash, Sarah, illustrator.
Identifiers: Canadiana 20200389491 | ISBN 9781525301179 (hardcover)
Subjects: LCSH: Springer, 1999 or 2000– | LCSH: Killer whale — Juvenile literature.
Classification: LCC QL737.C432 S26 2021 | DDC j599.53/6 — dc23

Kids Can Press gratefully acknowledges that the land on which our office is located is the traditional territory of many nations, including the Mississaugas of the Credit, the Anishnabeg, the Chippewa, the Haudenosaunee and the Wendat peoples, and is now home to many diverse First Nations, Inuit and Métis peoples.

We thank the Government of Ontario, through Ontario Creates; the Ontario Arts Council; the Canada Council for the Arts; and the Government of Canada for supporting our publishing activity.

ORCA RESCUE!

THE TRUE STORY OF AN ORPHANED ORCA NAMED SPRINGER

Written by **DONNA SANDSTROM**

Illustrated by **SARAH BURWASH**

Kids Can Press

Contents

Foreword

Phwoosh! A male orca surfaced near me in Blackfish Sound, where I was seeing orcas in the wild for the first time. It was 1985 and I had come to British Columbia to learn about them. The huge male came up so close I could smell his fishy breath. His tall dorsal fin glistened in the sun. "That," said the researcher standing beside me, "is as good as it gets."

I grew up in California near the beach, and loved seeing whales and dolphins. Sometimes we saw gray whales spouting close to shore. But my interest in orcas began when I moved to Seattle and started dreaming about them.

In the first dream, I was looking at a map of the Strait of Juan de Fuca. Suddenly 80 dorsal fins burst through the map, and the water became real. I was hovering overhead looking down on a large group of killer whales, headed east.

I woke with a start. Who were these whales and what were they doing in my dreams?

I started reading everything I could. I learned that orcas live in close families called pods and stay with their mothers their entire lives. That they are not whales but the largest member of the dolphin family — playful, curious and intelligent. And though they are the top predator in the sea, they can be as gentle as they are fierce. The more I learned, the more I wanted to know.

Soon I was spending every vacation traveling to see whales. In 1992, I went to Hawaii for a conference about whales and dolphins. Researcher Paul Spong gave a presentation about orcas. I knew people in Seattle would love it, so I asked Paul if he would give the talk there. He said yes! When I got home, I had to learn how to put on a public event — something I'd never done before. My friends and I formed a group called Orca Alliance. We rented a hall and made posters.

Near where I live, there is an outdoor pool with a pool house. During winter when the pool was closed, someone had taped photos of orcas to the pool house windows. I slipped a poster under the door, hoping whoever took the pictures would find it.

The night of the presentation, I met Mark Sears, the pool caretaker. He grew up on Puget Sound watching orcas and became a part-time whale researcher. When whales are near, he takes photos to identify them and records their behaviors. We have been friends ever since.

In 1993, I started working at a software company, an exciting place where I learned how to manage projects and teams. And through it all, I wrote — poems and stories and journals, where I kept track of my orca dreams.

The strands of my life came together in 2002, when a young orca was discovered alone near the north end of Vashon Island. This is the true story of what happened next.

She Arrives

January 2002

When the little whale showed up, no one knew who she was. A quartermaster on the Vashon ferry called my friend Mark Sears and told him there was a young orca swimming nearby. Mark was skeptical. He hadn't heard of any whales in the area.

"It's an orca for sure," the quartermaster said. "And it looks like she's alone."

Weird, Mark thought. Orcas live in tightly bonded families called **pods**. They stay with their mothers their entire lives. In more than 30 years of studying whales near Seattle, Mark had never encountered an orca by itself — especially a young one.

But the quartermaster was a reliable spotter, so Mark decided to go out and have a look.

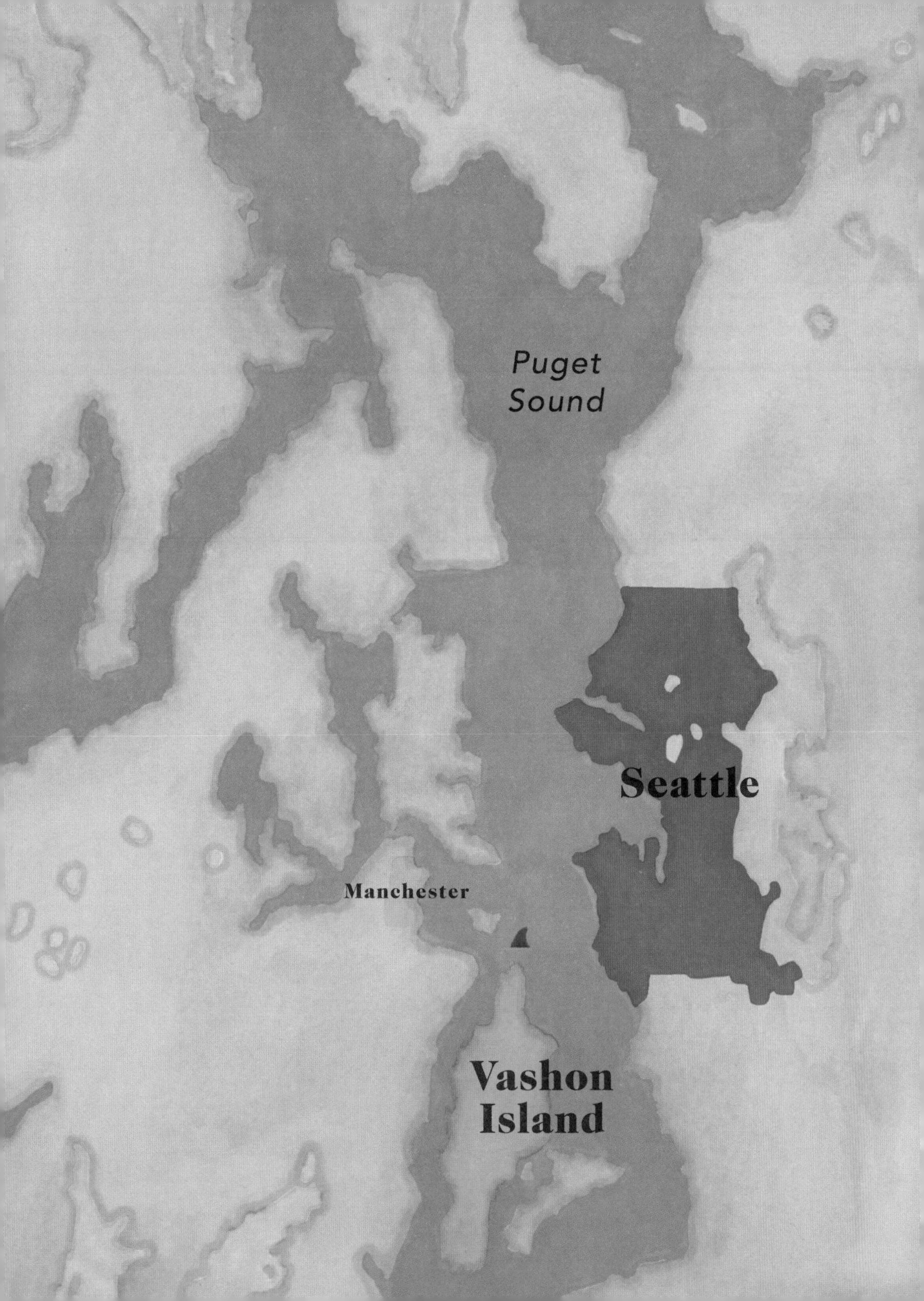

Puget
Sound

Seattle

Manchester

Vashon
Island

As he got dressed to go out on the water, Mark wondered if this animal could be a Dall's porpoise. They are black and white and are sometimes mistaken for orcas, even though they're much smaller.

It was a cold, clear afternoon, and the water was calm and glassy. Mark launched his skiff and headed west toward Vashon Island. He stopped every so often to scan through binoculars for a **blow**, the spout of water made by a whale when it exhales.

Halfway between Seattle and Vashon, Mark spotted what looked like a little **dorsal fin** slicing through the water. He lifted his binoculars and zoomed in for a closer look. Definitely not a porpoise! From the fin's shape and size, he could tell it was an orca.

Then he focused on the orca's back, looking for the white mark just behind the dorsal fin. Every orca has a white mark, called a **saddle patch**, that is unique, like a human fingerprint. It's one of the main ways to tell orcas apart. But Mark couldn't find a saddle patch on this little whale. Its skin was gray and blotchy, covered with bumps.

Whoever this whale was, it seemed to be in a hurry, charging toward … what, exactly? Mark trained the binoculars in the direction the orca was going, and saw a big tree stump bobbing in the water.

Sure enough, the little orca headed right for the stump and rubbed up against it. Mark slowed down and moved the boat closer to get a better look. The whale was using the stump like a giant back scratcher! The orca rubbed — first its back, then its side — against the branches, as if it had a big itch.

When the whale rolled over, Mark saw the white marking on its underside. Aha! From the shape of the white mark, he could tell this was a female orca. Judging by her size, he estimated she was about two years old.

A young orca, alone, with a hard-to-see saddle patch and no family nearby. Now Mark was *really* curious. What was she doing here? And where was her pod?

All about Orcas

Orcas, also called **killer whales**, are the largest member of the dolphin family. They are **cetaceans**, which means they belong to the family of marine mammals that includes whales, dolphins and porpoises. This illustration shows an adult female orca.

Like all dolphins, orcas are curious, playful and intelligent. They are acoustic animals, which means they use sound to navigate and communicate. Some use **echolocation**, a focused stream of clicks, to find and hunt their prey.

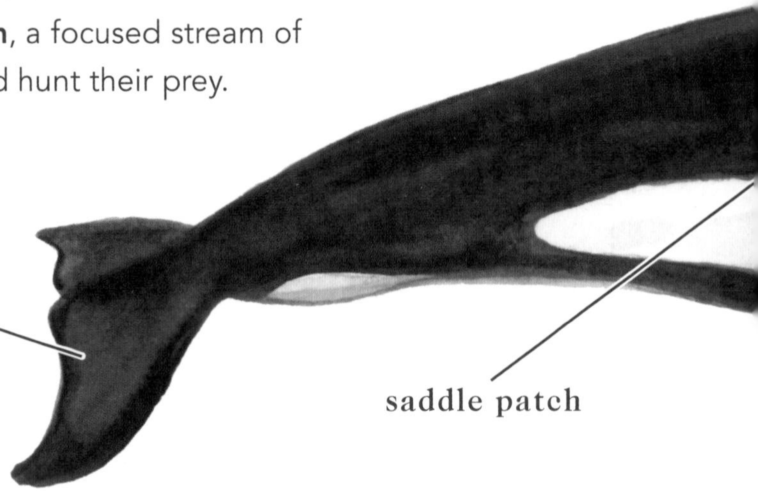

tail flukes

saddle patch

Orcas are the top predator in the sea — nothing hunts an orca! Because they are smart and fast, and work together to catch their prey, they are sometimes called the wolves of the sea. What they eat and how they hunt are cultural, taught to them by their families.

Some orcas eat marine mammals, such as seals, porpoises or whales. Others eat fish, such as salmon, herring or even sharks. Hunting strategies, like washing a seal off an ice floe or flipping a shark upside down, may be taught, practiced and learned.

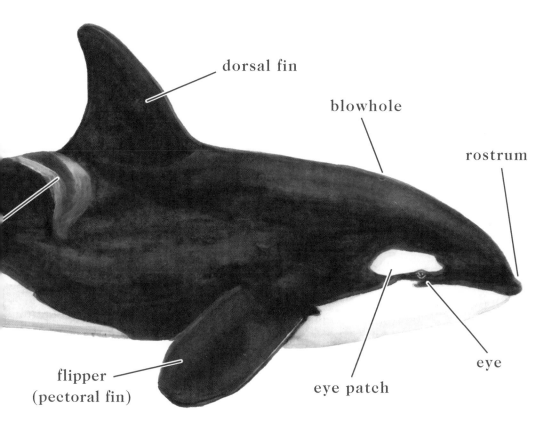

dorsal fin

blowhole

rostrum

flipper
(pectoral fin)

eye patch

eye

Orcas' black and white markings and tall dorsal fins make them easy to spot. Dorsal fins can grow as high as 1.8 m (6 ft.) on a male and 0.6 to 0.9 m (2 to 3 ft.) high on a female. The shape of the fin and markings, such as cuts and scars, can be used to tell orcas apart.

Orcas are found in every ocean. In the Pacific Northwest, there are three **ecotypes**, or kinds, of orcas with different habitats, diets and family structures.

Resident orcas eat fish such as salmon, and they like Chinook salmon best of all. They live in large, stable pods organized around the mothers, or **matriarchs**. When you see a resident pod, you might see four generations of whales traveling together! Two populations of resident orcas live in the Pacific Northwest. Northern resident orcas live around the north end of Vancouver Island, and southern resident orcas live around the south end.

Bigg's orcas (also called transient orcas) hunt marine mammals, such as seals and porpoises. Small family groups travel along the Pacific Coast and the inland waters of the Salish Sea. Their range, or the area where they live, is wider than that of resident orcas, and their travel patterns are less predictable.

Offshore orcas are fish-eaters who live in the deep ocean. They are rarely seen near the coast.

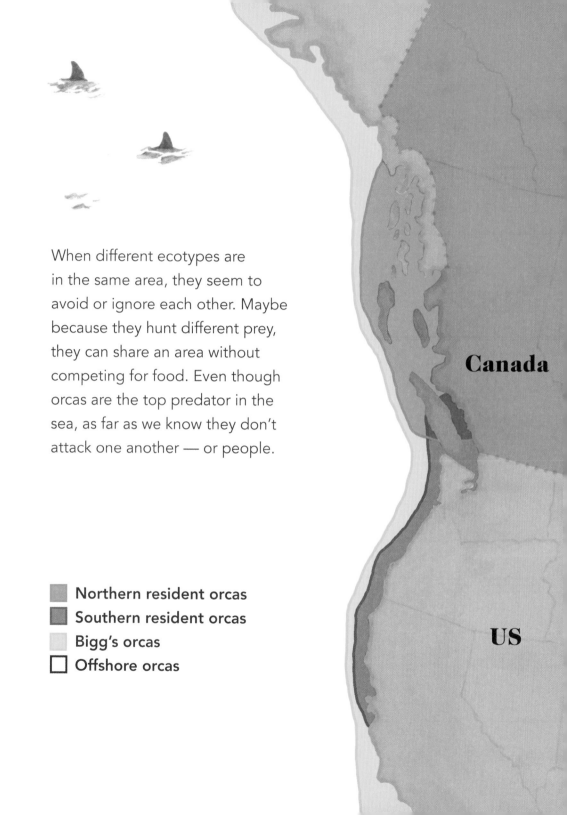

When different ecotypes are in the same area, they seem to avoid or ignore each other. Maybe because they hunt different prey, they can share an area without competing for food. Even though orcas are the top predator in the sea, as far as we know they don't attack one another — or people.

Canada

US

■ Northern resident orcas
■ Southern resident orcas
□ Bigg's orcas
☐ Offshore orcas

Who's That Whale?

January 2002

Mark phoned a government scientist and told him about the mystery whale. News spread quickly among the small community of orca researchers. Over the next few days, Mark took many of them out to see her.

The little orca had settled into an area near the north end of Vashon Island. When researchers wanted to look at her close up, Mark had one sure way to bring her near the boat. All he had to do was hold up a stick and wave it. From wherever she was, she would come charging toward the stick, like a puppy! He'd throw her the stick and she'd play with it, while researchers took notes.

One day I went out with Mark to check on the little orca. Before we even spotted her, I picked up a piece of wood that was floating nearby. From halfway across the Sound, she saw what I'd done and swam straight toward us.

"What should I do?" I asked, in a panic.

"You'd better give it to her!" Mark said with a laugh.

I tossed the stick into the water. She grabbed it with her mouth and flipped it onto her back. Then she rolled over and balanced it on her belly. She was having a lot of fun with that stick!

She dove again. When I looked down, she was under the boat, looking up at me. Our eyes met for a few seconds. Then, she slowly drifted down into the inky sea.

Researchers had different ideas about who she might be. Was she a Bigg's orca or even an offshore? Her saddle patch couldn't be used to identify her, but maybe her calls would help.

In the 1980s, marine biologist John Ford discovered that resident pods have unique calls. Just by listening, scientists can tell which pod a resident orca belongs to. Some pods' calls sound like creaking doors. Others sound like donkeys!

Researchers went out with Mark to record the little whale using an underwater microphone called a **hydrophone**. At first, they heard "baby talk," sounds that any young orca might make. Then suddenly — surprise! She made a call used only by a northern resident pod called the A4s. It was like she was saying, "I am an A4 orca!" She repeated the call, as if she wanted to be sure they heard.

The A4s are a well-known pod with a sad history. In 1983, the matriarch, or female leader of the pod, was shot and killed in Johnstone Strait, along with her youngest calf. They were likely killed by a fisherman who saw them as competition for salmon.

The matriarch (known as A10) had two other daughters, Kelsey and Yakat. Almost 20 years later, the little orca was making a call that could have come only from one of their families.

News of the whale's call spread quickly. Researchers combed through their files to see if any calves were missing from Kelsey's or Yakat's pod.

At OrcaLab on Hanson Island, Paul Spong and Helena Symonds checked their notes. Paul and Helena have been recording orcas in the Johnstone Strait area since 1979. They keep track of which whales have been there and when.

Their notes showed that in the summer of 2000, Kelsey and Yakat had returned to the strait with their families. One of Kelsey's daughters, Sutlej, had a new calf, Springer.

The next year when the families returned, Springer and her mother were missing. When orcas disappear, it usually means they have died. It's hard to know when or why, since their bodies are rarely found. Young calves who lose their mothers typically don't survive.

Graeme Ellis, another Canadian researcher, found a photo of Springer as a calf. He compared her eye patch to a photo of the little whale in Seattle. They matched exactly. There was no question now — the little whale was Springer. She was still alive! But what was she doing on her own, so far away from home?

Researchers tried to fit the pieces together like a giant jigsaw puzzle. An American scientist found a picture of Springer with her mother in Ketchikan, Alaska, in September 2000 — the last time they were seen together.

Then Graeme found a picture of Springer with a different pod called the G1s. In 2001, the G1s had been spotted near the entrance of the Strait of Juan de Fuca, a body of water that connects the Pacific Ocean to the Salish Sea.

The puzzle pieces fell into place. Springer had somehow survived the death of her mother. She joined up with the G1s and traveled south with them. At some point, she became separated from them and swam alone into the Strait of Juan de Fuca. Was she following a salmon? Did she think she was entering her home waters of Johnstone Strait?

We'll never know for sure. We do know that Springer swam into Puget Sound toward Seattle. She settled into one of the busiest waterways, and best fishing grounds, in the area.

The mystery of who she was had been solved. Springer was a northern resident orca. Her mother had died, but her grandmother, great-aunt and cousins were still alive in Canada. Now there was another big question to answer: What should we do?

The Resident Orcas

The Pacific Northwest's resident orcas are among the most well-studied animals in the world. In the 1970s, marine biologist Mike Bigg learned how to tell orcas apart by comparing photos of their dorsal fins and saddle patches — a method called photo-identification. Today the life history of almost every resident orca is known.

How Are Resident Orcas Named?
Each orca is given a letter for its pod and a number for its order in the pod. Springer is A73, meaning she's the 73rd orca born in A pod since researchers started keeping track. Orcas are also given a nickname, such as Springer, Yakat or Kelsey.

Where Do Resident Orcas Live?

Northern resident orcas live around the north end of Vancouver Island and along the central British Columbia coast. They travel as far north as southeast Alaska and as far south as the Washington coast. During summer, they usually return to Johnstone Strait.

Southern resident orcas live around the south end of Vancouver Island and along the Pacific Coast, as far south as Monterey Bay, California. They return to the Salish Sea each summer, and hunt for salmon in central Puget Sound during the winter.

How Many Resident Orcas Are There?

In 2019, there were about 300 northern resident orcas, in 26 pods. The northern resident population is steadily growing. Sadly, the number of southern resident orcas is shrinking. In 2019, there were just 73 orcas in 3 pods. The southern resident population is critically endangered.

Resident Orca Culture

Just like humans, orcas have cultures, which means they have patterns of shared, learned behaviors. Northern and southern resident orcas have similar cultures, even though they are not biologically related.

Calls: Resident orcas use special calls to communicate with each other. They learn the calls from their families. Some calls are shared only with their families, and some are shared with other pods, too.

Kelping: Southern resident orcas like to swim through kelp beds and drape the long leaves over their flippers, heads and bellies. It probably feels good against their skin.

Prey-sharing: When resident orcas catch a fish, they don't just gobble it down — they share it with one another. Researchers are just starting to discover the rules for sharing. Mothers share salmon with their sons and daughters, until the daughters have their own calves. And adult males share food with their mothers.

Rubbing: Northern resident orcas visit shallow beaches and roll their bodies across smooth stones. They take turns at the beaches, pod by pod, like family visits to a pebbly spa.

Superpod: Sometimes many groups of orcas come together in a large social gathering called a superpod. They may stay together for days, hunting, resting and playing.

Orcas are conservative, meaning they don't easily make cultural changes. For example, mammal-eating orcas don't eat fish, and fish-eating orcas don't eat mammals.

What Should We Do?

February–April 2002

Springer was lost, alone and more than 482 km (300 mi.) away from home. Without human help, there was no way she would find her way back to her family. Making things even more complicated, she was stranded in the United States, but her home and her family were in Canada. The two countries would need to work together.

The **National Oceanic and Atmospheric Administration** (NOAA) is responsible for the health of whales and dolphins in the United States. The **Department of Fisheries and Oceans** (DFO) has the same role in Canada. The agencies formed a team to help Springer. The team was led by Joe Scordino from NOAA. Biologists and veterinarians from both countries would advise the decision-makers.

Over the next few weeks, researchers observed Springer. On the plus side, she seemed to have a lot of energy and was even seen breaching, or leaping out of the water. She was also catching salmon on her own — an amazing accomplishment for an orca her age. Normally, young orcas work with their families to find fish, and they share with one another.

But Springer was underweight. There was a sunken area behind her **blowhole**. In healthy whales, this area is smooth and round, like a plump olive. When whales start losing weight, the area behind the blowhole sinks. This can be a serious sign that an orca is sick.

And there was another sign that something was wrong. When Springer exhaled, her breath smelled like acetone, or nail polish remover. That is a symptom of a condition called **ketosis** and could mean that she was starving. When animals are super hungry, they may digest their own fat, which produces acetone and makes their breath smell like Springer's. Only further medical tests could determine how sick she was and if she could be treated.

Researchers were worried about Springer's social health, too. She had been on her own for a long time. Without other orcas around, she would look to people for company. This was risky and dangerous — she could be injured, or even killed, by boats and their propellers.

Springer was already attracting a lot of attention. She liked to rest near the Vashon ferry dock, and people rode the ferry just to see her. Some even tried to feed her, tossing french fries at her, as if she were a pet.

NOAA put up signs asking people to leave her alone. Enforcement boats kept people away from her on weekends. But Joe knew these were only temporary solutions. As the weather got warmer, Puget Sound would become more crowded, and the risks to Springer would only increase.

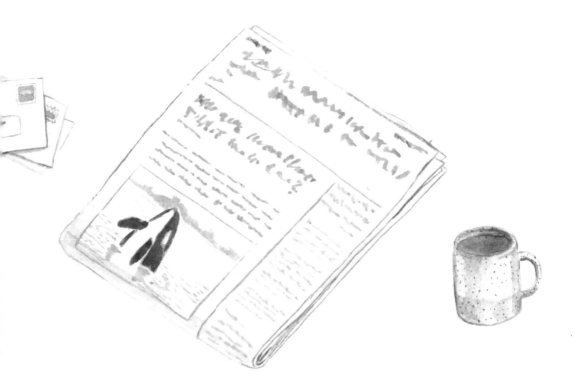

Joe knew they had to do something. But what? Before he decided, he wanted to hear from the community. He asked Kathy Fletcher, the leader of a local environmental group, to set up a public meeting.

On the night of the meeting, the hall was packed. Every seat was taken, and camera crews crowded the aisles. My friend Peggy and I got there early. She was part of Orca Alliance and loved orcas as much as I did. Like everyone in the room, we were worried about what would happen to Springer.

Joe said that NOAA was considering four options:

1. Do nothing.

They would leave Springer alone where she was.

2. Send Springer to an aquarium.

She would be taken care of, but she would never see her family or live as a wild whale again.

3. Rehabilitate her in an aquarium.

She would be sent to an aquarium for medical tests and treatment. If she was healthy, they would try to take her back to Canada.

4. Rehabilitate her in Puget Sound, which is called in situ rehabilitation.

This was the same as option three, except that Springer would be moved to a location in Puget Sound instead of an aquarium so she could be kept as wild as possible. If she was healthy, the team would try to take her home.

Every option was risky and expensive. Plus, no one had ever successfully returned a wild orca to its pod. Joe asked what the audience thought NOAA should do. Before making their decision, NOAA wanted to hear from us.

First, the scientists weighed in. They said that Springer was probably sick and should be sent to an aquarium, soon. Many people in the audience agreed.

A young boy was the first person to say that Springer might not be sick but lost. "And if she is lost," he said, "she should get to go home. Her family probably misses her. Send her back to them!" The crowd clapped loudly.

When it was my turn, I agreed with him. "Give Springer a chance to go home. If she goes to an aquarium, she may never come out. Pick the in situ option and we will support you."

When the meeting was over, Peggy and I introduced ourselves to Joe. We told him we were serious. "If you treat her in Puget Sound, our group and others will help you."

Joe was intrigued. "This has never been done before," he said. "We can try our best, but we don't know how it will turn out. Will you take the risk with us?"

"Yes!" Peggy and I both said.

Three weeks later at a meeting on Vashon Island, NOAA announced they had made a decision. NOAA, DFO and the Vancouver Aquarium would try to rescue Springer and return her to her family. And they had chosen the in situ rehabilitation, just as we had hoped!

Springer would be moved to a **net pen** in Puget Sound near Manchester, Washington, for medical tests and treatment. She would be looked after by an experienced team of marine mammal veterinarians. Specially trained handlers would help with the physical tasks, such as moving her into and out of the pen.

If Springer was healthy, she would be returned to Johnstone Strait by midsummer, when her pod was most likely to be there. Then, everyone hoped, she'd be released and reunited with her family.

On the ferry back to West Seattle, Peggy and I stood on the deck, happy and nervous at the same time. Our thoughts churned like the water in the ferry's wake. Springer was out there, somewhere in the dark. Her life, and ours, were about to change.

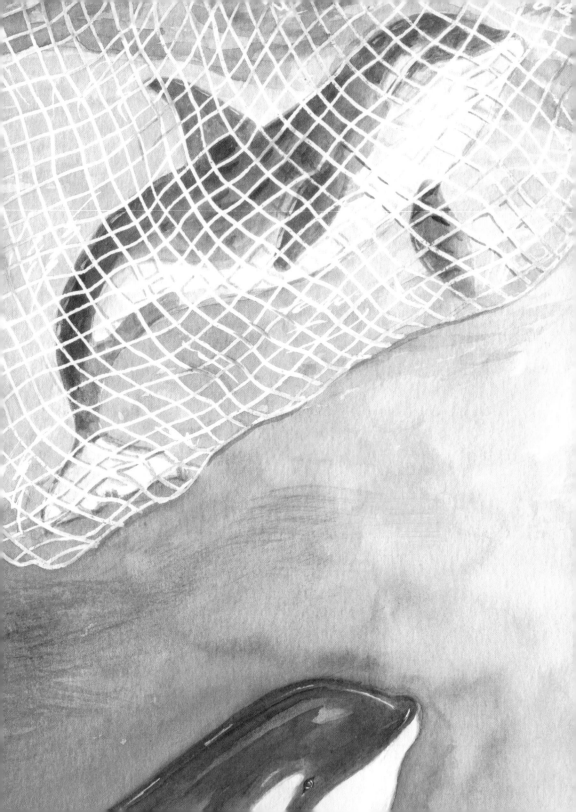

Orcas in Captivity

The Capture Era

Before the 1960s, orcas had never been put on public display. That changed in 1964, when the Vancouver Aquarium got an orca by mistake.

The aquarium wanted a sculpture of an orca, and their artist decided to use a dead one as a model. He went to a nearby island, and when a pod approached, he harpooned the smallest whale. Only, the orca didn't die.

The wounded orca was towed to Vancouver and nicknamed "Moby Doll." Everyone thought Moby Doll would be fierce, like a shark. Instead, the orca was playful and gentle. Hundreds of people came to see him, and other aquariums offered to buy him. Moby Doll lived just a few months more, but his capture changed the fate of orcas forever.

In 1965, a male orca was caught in fishing nets near Namu, British Columbia. A Seattle businessman, Ted Griffin, bought the orca and towed him to a pen on the Seattle waterfront. He charged five dollars for each person to see "Namu," and thousands of people came. A devastating new industry was born.

Ted and his business partner began capturing and selling orcas to marine parks around the world. Over the next 10 years, they separated dozens of orcas from their families.

Change Begins

In 1976, former Washington Secretary of State Ralph Munro saw orcas being captured near Olympia. The captors dropped noise bombs in the water to frighten and herd the whales. Ralph was shocked by what he saw. Washington State sued the federal government to stop the captures, and won.

With orcas safe in Washington, the captors moved on to other places, such as Iceland, Japan, Russia and Argentina.

By the time the captures were stopped, more than 60 orcas had been captured or had died during the attempts. Most of the whales sold to aquariums died within a few years.

The captures removed more than one-third of the southern resident population, including most of the calves and young mothers, from the wild. That catastrophic loss is one of the reasons that the southern residents are endangered today.

Rescue!

April–May 2002

Now that the decision was made, the team got ready to move Springer. NOAA needed supplies and donations for both Springer and her caretakers. Joe asked Orca Alliance if we would help. Peggy and I said yes. Six other groups said yes, too.

Surprisingly, one group said no. They were afraid that something would go wrong, and so they didn't want to be part of it. The rest of us knew that for the best to happen — for Springer to be with her family — we had to risk that worse things could happen, too.

Orcas are sensitive, intelligent animals. By surviving on her own for so long, Springer had shown that she was smart and strong. But no one knew how she would react to the stress of being captured or living in a small pen.

Another risk was that, after she was captured, veterinarians might discover that she was sick with something that couldn't be treated. Then she would likely not be released back to the wild and would stay in permanent human care. No one wanted that, but it was a risk we had to take to reunite her with her family.

Peggy and I met with the other groups and decided what to call ourselves. The **Orphan Orca Fund** was born!

Joe needed help for his team, too. Getting Springer home would take a lot of time and people. Lynne Barre worked at NOAA's headquarters in Washington, D.C. She came out to Seattle to help.

Lynne gave the Orphan Orca Fund a long list of supplies that NOAA needed for the rescue: a foam pad for Springer to rest on, a scale to weigh her, medical equipment and more. They also needed ferry passes, groceries and scuba tanks for Springer's caretakers … and portable toilets, too!

Over the next week, we called companies all around Seattle. It was like being on a giant scavenger hunt. Everyone had heard of Springer, and everyone wanted to help. Within a few weeks, we had almost everything NOAA needed.

Before setting a date for the rescue, Joe wanted to know if Springer had any diseases that would keep her from going home. Dr. Pete Schroeder, a marine mammal veterinarian, said they could take a blood sample to find out.

There was just one small problem — no one had ever taken a blood sample from a free-swimming whale! It's hard enough to get people to sit still for a doctor or nurse. How do you persuade an orca?

With her stick, of course! The team used Springer's stick to call her close to the boat. When she turned on her side, Dr. Pete tried to put a needle into her **tail fluke**. Springer flinched and swam away, but luckily, she came back. He put the needle in her dorsal fin and got the sample they needed.

It took a week for the results to come back from the lab. We waited nervously … Would Springer's journey end before it started? But the news was good. Springer didn't have any of the diseases the team was most worried about.

Marine mammal handler Jeff Foster started working with Springer to get her used to the team and the equipment they would use. The rescue date was set for May 13.

May 13, 2002

Rescue day was sunny and clear. Reporters crowded onto a press boat while news helicopters hovered noisily overhead. The eyes of the world were on Springer.

The team got into place — Jeff and his team on a small boat near Springer, and everyone else on a wide, flat barge. Security boats kept the area clear for about 3 km (2 mi.) in every direction.

Jeff got into the water with Springer to load her into the sling. When she was secure, he gave a thumbs-up to the crane operator. Slowly, slowly, she was lifted out of the water. Her little fins poked out of the sling — it looked like she was flying! The crane swiveled over to the barge and lowered her onto a soft foam mattress.

The crossing to Manchester would take 30 minutes. Even in that short time, anything could go wrong. It isn't natural for orcas to be out of the water. They need the buoyancy of seawater to support their heavy bodies. Springer could panic or become overheated.

Jeff talked to her to keep her calm. Dr. Pete measured her temperature, heartbeat and breathing. Joe, Lynne and other members of the NOAA team filled buckets with seawater to pour over her and keep her cool.

When the barge reached Manchester, the crane lifted Springer and lowered her into the pen. Then she dove and started exploring her new home.

Whale Behaviors

Have you ever seen a whale breach? The huge mammals jump out of the water and come down with a huge splash, thrilling anyone lucky enough to see. If whales breach once, they are likely to do it again. And sometimes, one breaching whale will inspire another, and the sea becomes filled with leaping whales.

Why do whales breach? It might be a kind of communication. Or it might just be as fun as it looks. We know a lot about what orcas do, but it's harder to say why they do it — especially since most of what we see is on the surface.

Breaching: when an orca leaps completely out of the water and comes back down with a big splash

Pectoral Slap: when an orca lifts its **pectoral fin** (or flipper) and slaps it against the surface of the water, creating a loud sound

Porpoising: when an orca swims so fast that some or all of its body breaks the surface of the water

Resting Line: when orca families nestle close to one another and swim together slowly

Like all whales and dolphins, orcas are conscious breathers. They have to stay alert to breathe, so they never fall completely asleep. A resting line is their version of sleeping.

Spyhopping: when a whale or dolphin sticks its head out of the water to look around

Tail Lobbing: when a whale slaps its tail flukes against the surface of the water, creating a loud sound

On the Mend

June 2002

Springer's rescue had gone as planned. Now she would be tested to see if she was healthy enough to go home. No one knew how long that would take, but the team didn't want her to spend more than a few weeks in the small net pen. She would lose muscle tone and stamina every day she was confined. In the wild, orcas may swim 113 to 161 km (70 to 100 mi.) each day. If Springer was going to rejoin her pod, she needed to be able to keep up with them.

The team also didn't want her to lose the skills she already had, like hunting and catching fish on her own. Most of all, they didn't want her to get too attached to people. No matter how long she was in their care, she needed to remember that orcas, not people, were her family. Springer needed to stay as wild as possible.

The team found creative ways to keep Springer active, hunting and wild.

Limited contact with people. Springer was already used to the medical staff and handlers. They were the only people who were allowed to have direct contact with her. A high cloth barrier was placed around her pen so that she wouldn't see or interact with anyone on the dock.

Remote monitoring. The team put cameras in Springer's pen so they could watch her 24 hours a day. They monitored her from a guardhouse next to the pen. If anything went wrong, they would know right away. Dr. Pete was always on call.

Natural toys. Orcas are playful and curious, and Springer would get bored in the small pen. The team gave her toys to play with, but only things she would find in the wild, such as kelp, streams of water … and her stick! They hoped her stick would make her feel comfortable, like a familiar blanket.

Salmon waterslide! The team didn't want Springer to associate food with people. Live salmon were slipped down a feeding tube that emptied into her pen. They loaded the salmon at random times so she wouldn't get used to eating on a schedule.

But Springer was a smart little orca. She waited by the tube for salmon to pop out!

When Springer arrived at Manchester, she was about 3.4 m (11 ft.) long and weighed 562 kg (1240 lb.) — much bigger than a human but a little smaller than other orcas her age. Dr. Pete and the other veterinarians took more samples of her blood, blow (exhaled breath) and feces (poop). They hoped to find out what was causing her skin condition. And they had to be sure she wasn't carrying a disease that could spread to other orcas.

The blood sample took a week to process. The results were good! The tests were repeated to make sure the results were the same. With so much at risk for the wild orca population, no one wanted to make a mistake.

Springer's **fecal samples** showed she had a bad case of worms. Just like dogs and cats, orcas can get parasites in their intestines, and Springer had a lot of them. Dr. Pete gave her two treatments of deworming medicine — the first-ever deworming of a wild whale. Right away, Springer started getting better. She went from eating two salmon a day to fifteen!

While Springer settled in, the Orphan Orca Fund kept working. A store in Seattle donated fruit and snacks for the team. Peggy and I brought the groceries to Manchester. Lynne took us out to the guardhouse. On the monitors, we watched Springer play with little bits of kelp. She picked up the pieces with her teeth and dropped them, then swooped to catch them again.

We laughed and then got a little teary. It had been only a few months since that first meeting with Joe. Now everything we'd talked about that night was coming true. Springer was getting a chance to go home.

The next weekend, we set up a donation table at the Seattle Aquarium. A steady stream of people put coins in Springer's jar. A mother helped her daughter, and I thought about Springer's family. Did they know she was still alive?

Dong
Chong
Bay

Alert Bay

Hanson
Island

Telegraph
Cove

Springer was getting healthier every day. Once she was dewormed, she put on weight, and her skin started to clear up, too. The Canadian team got ready for her to come home.

Springer would be carried by boat from Seattle to Johnstone Strait — a trip that would take all day. She would be held in a net pen for up to two weeks and released when her family was near. Of course, there was no guarantee her family would return within that time. If they didn't, she would be released when other orcas were around.

Where should they put the pen? They looked for a deep bay, in a place where Springer's family could find her.

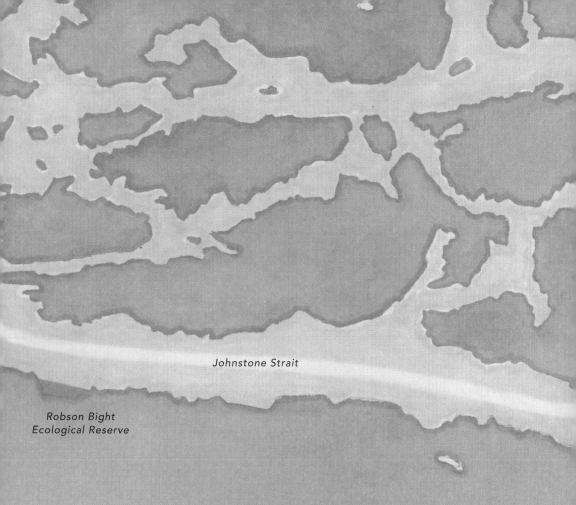

Johnstone Strait

Robson Bight
Ecological Reserve

They picked Dong Chong Bay on the north side of Hanson Island, in 'Namgis First Nation traditional territory. The bay was big enough to hold the pen, and it was in the heart of the orcas' summer range. Her family would be sure to see and hear Springer when — or *if* — they swam by.

Plus, Dong Chong Bay was next to OrcaLab. Their hydrophones would let everyone know when orcas were in the area.

Back in Seattle, NOAA faced a new challenge. The ship that was supposed to carry Springer home was called away on a different mission. NOAA needed to find a new boat — and fast. Joe asked the Orphan Orca Fund and other community members if we knew anyone who had a boat big enough for Springer and her team.

After a lot of phone calls, a shipbuilder on Whidbey Island offered to provide a high-speed **catamaran** and a captain for it, too! Once again, the community came through for Springer.

The Orphan Orca Fund's work was almost done, and we had some money left over. Paul had a good idea about how to spend it. We hired a fishing boat from the 'Namgis First Nation to catch wild salmon for Springer and load it into her pen in Dong Chong Bay. There would be plenty of fresh fish waiting when she came home.

JULY

	1	2	3	4	5	6
7	8	9	10	11	(12)	13
14	15	16	17	18	19	20
21	22	23	24	25	26	27
28	29	30	31			

The results from the last round of medical tests came back clear, and the veterinarians gave Springer the green light to go home. July 12 would be the day.

Free Keiko

The movie *Free Willy* tells the fictional story of a young boy who frees an orca from an aquarium. The star of the movie was a real orca named Keiko, who lived at an aquarium in Mexico City. Keiko had been captured in Iceland in 1979, when he was only a young calf.

The movie inspired children around the world to ask for Keiko's freedom. They wrote thousands of letters to the movie producers and the aquarium's owner. And they got their wish! In 1995, the Free Willy/Keiko Foundation was formed to return Keiko to the wild.

Keiko was moved from Mexico City to a bigger aquarium in Newport, Oregon. There, he relearned the skills he would need to live in the ocean, such as how to hunt and catch live fish. Two years later, the team moved Keiko to a net pen in Iceland. They trained him to follow their boat and took him for exercise "walks" in the ocean.

Unlike with Springer, no one knew who Keiko's family was, so he couldn't be returned to them. The team hoped he would join a local pod. In 2002, Keiko was released to live on his own.

A few months later, Keiko swam across the ocean to a fjord in Norway. He met other orcas but never fully bonded with them. Keiko settled in a bay near a small town and interacted with people there, turning to humans for companionship. He died in 2003.

Although his story didn't end as anyone had hoped, Keiko had a taste of freedom, and the team learned a lot from the effort to return him to the wild. Orca societies are complex. If Keiko could have been returned to his family, maybe his chances would have been better.

Some of the experts who worked with Keiko, like Jeff Foster, were hired to work with Springer. The lessons they learned from Keiko were put to good use for her.

Heading North

July 12, 2002

On Friday July 12, we all got up early.

I drove north towards Canada with friends from the Orphan Orca Fund. We wanted to be there when Springer came home. On the ferry to Vancouver Island, we overheard people talking about Springer. Her picture was on the front page of all the papers. We suddenly realized this was a big story in Canada, too. Everyone's hearts were with the little orca, hoping for the best.

Meanwhile, Kathy and other members of the Orphan Orca Fund went to Manchester. They wanted to wave goodbye to Springer and her team and wish them well on their journey. They waited and waited … and waited … but the catamaran never came. Finally, someone told them that the boat had mechanical problems and the trip was postponed. Springer would have to wait another day to go home.

**Orphan orca will hop
a boat home Friday**

The boat crew fixed the problem, and the next day, the catamaran arrived right on time. The team loaded Springer into her sling, and the crane lifted her over to the boat. While she was in the sling, she was weighed. Springer had gained over 45 kg (100 lb.) in the 30 days she was at Manchester!

The crane lowered Springer into a transport box filled with cold seawater. When she was settled, the boat left the dock. Kathy and the other members of the Orphan Orca Fund watched and waved as the boat pulled away.

At the Vashon ferry dock, a dance group of **First Nations** people and **Native Americans** sang to Springer as she passed by. The sound of their drums carried across the water like a heartbeat. The catamaran glided over the spot where Springer had been discovered just six months earlier. Then the captain turned north, toward Canada.

On board the boat, Springer seemed scared at first and whimpered. Jeff talked to her and patted her, and she settled down. The team measured her heartbeat, temperature and breathing rate, as they would throughout the trip. To make her comfortable, a special toy came with her. The team had brought her stick!

When the boat crossed the United States–Canada border, responsibility for Springer shifted to the Canadian team, who now took the lead.

As the trip went on, the water in Springer's transport box was getting warm, and the team was running out of ice to cool it down. They decided to stop in Campbell River, a city on Vancouver Island, for more. When they docked, it seemed the whole town was waiting to greet them. The We Wai Kai Nation even presented the captain with a carved mask.

They got plenty of ice for Springer, plus pizza for the humans, and the journey north went on.

HOME OF THE KILLER WHALE

SPRINGER

WELCOME
HOME
SPRINGER

WELCOME
HOME

Homecoming

July 13, 2002

While Springer was headed north, my friends and I were in Alert Bay, a village on an island near where she would be released. Alert Bay is part of the traditional territory of the Kwakwaka'wakw and is known as the "Home of the Killer Whale." We saw signs that said Welcome Home Springer.

We planned to watch the catamaran pass by from a lookout on a cliff high above Johnstone Strait. Our friend Rob, a local researcher, would take us there in his boat. First, we went shopping for lunch supplies.

At the grocery store, I met a woman named Cecilia, who was wearing a vest embroidered with a killer whale design. She told me she was from the Whale Clan and that they were having a feast to welcome Springer home.

"I'm here because of Springer!" I told her. "We have been working on the project, and I came from Seattle just to be here."

Cecilia's eyes filled with tears. "When I heard she was coming back, I wanted to be sure her family knows. Last night I went down to the beach and called the whales in the old way. I haven't done that in a long, long time. Granny, I said, you'd better get here, your granddaughter is coming home!"

Now my eyes were filled with tears, too. Wherever she was, I hoped Springer's grandmother had heard Cecilia's call.

We stopped to visit friends whose boat was anchored in Dong Chong Bay. They invited us to come aboard and watch Springer come home with them. Instead of being on a faraway cliff, we would have front-row seats in the bay!

The area around the net pen was closed to the public. The rest of the bay was filling up with fishing boats, pleasure boats and kayaks — Springer's welcoming party! All through the afternoon, boats arrived and anchored in the bay, while smaller boats carried people to the cedar-lined shore. People were having picnics while they waited, just like us. After lunch, we painted a banner that said Welcome Home Springer. She was getting closer with every hour that passed by.

Finally, a little after 5:30 p.m., the catamaran appeared at the entrance to the bay. Everyone started cheering as the tall white ship rounded the corner and came into view. Boaters blasted their horns.

On the shore of Hanson Island, dozens of people stood and started to sing. Women in red button blankets lifted their hands toward the catamaran. Drumming and women's high voices filled the bay.

A white canoe draped in cedar boughs headed toward the catamaran. The canoe carried a sign saying Welcome Baby Orka. The paddlers sang while a dancer in an orca mask swayed from side to side.

It was like being in a dream.

We watched through binoculars as Springer was lifted from the catamaran. We could see her pectoral fins poking through the sling as she flew through the air one last time. She was lowered onto a barge and brought closer to the pen, and the vets took a final round of measurements and samples. Then, the crane lifted her and lowered her into the water. Springer was home.

First Nations Chiefs waited to welcome her. 'Namgis Chief Bill Cranmer, wearing ceremonial regalia, leaned over and spoke to her in Kwak'wala. Springer spyhopped, as if she was listening. Then, she dove and started hunting.

We stayed on the boat until it was almost dark. As we made our way back to Rob's cabin, I wondered if Springer knew where she was. It had taken two countries and hundreds of people to make this moment happen. What happened next would be up to the whales.

Springer's team settled in for the first night's watch. Lance Barrett-Lennard, a research scientist from the Vancouver Aquarium, stayed in his boat near the pen. In the middle of the night, he heard faint, faraway calls on the hydrophones in Dong Chong Bay. Orcas!

Springer heard them, too. She called back excitedly. When the whales called again, you could almost hear a question mark in their voices, as if they were saying, *Who's that?*

Around the corner at OrcaLab, Paul and Helena were listening and recording. From their calls, they knew the orcas were related to Springer but were not her immediate family. The orcas called back and forth for hours. The whales swam closer and their calls got louder, rising and falling across the dark.

While Springer waited in her pen, her family was heading toward her. The next day, the team heard that the A4s had returned to the area overnight. Springer's grandmother, aunts and cousins were already in Blackfish Sound, headed toward Dong Chong Bay.

The team got ready. John and Graeme waited aboard a boat in Blackfish Sound, scanning for her family. Lance, Jeff and Dr. Pete were with Springer in the bay.

Springer's family came into view. When they got close to Dong Chong Bay, they slowed down, swam past the entrance and turned around. Then they lined up, facing Springer.

This was it! The moment everyone had been waiting for. No one could believe it had happened so fast. John waited to see how the orcas reacted to each other. Then, he radioed Lance to let her go.

Jeff and Dr. Pete lowered the net pen gate. Springer paused, long enough to catch a salmon. Then she bolted out toward her waiting family.

Of course, I didn't know any of this had happened. This was before everyone had cell phones! That same morning, I was in Telegraph Cove, having breakfast with my friends before they went back to Seattle. I would stay one more day.

Rob and I headed out to visit OrcaLab. Soon after we entered Blackfish Sound, he turned off the engine. "Orcas," he said, pointing east. I looked in the direction he was pointing, but I didn't see anything. We waited quietly, small waves lapping against the side of the boat. It is the most delicious feeling in the world, waiting for whales.

Rob looked through his binoculars. "There!" he said, pointing again. I trained my binoculars in the direction he was looking. "But that's not a group of orcas," he said. "It's just one. And it's a small one." His eyes grew wide. "I think it's … it's …"

"It's Springer!" I said. There was no mistaking that little whale. She must have been released!

As her little fin rose between the waves, I couldn't quite believe what I was seeing. Springer was swimming free in Blackfish Sound! I thought of everyone who'd worked so hard to make this moment happen. I wished so much they could see what I was seeing, too.

We watched for a while and then headed to OrcaLab to find out what had happened.

Together Again

July–August 2002

So much had gone right, but a lot could still go wrong. In those first few days, Springer had a hard time keeping up with her family. Even though she'd been in the pen for just a month, she had lost muscle tone and stamina. Everyone was worried.

Lance and other researchers kept a close eye on her. Just before Springer was released, they had placed a satellite tag on her back, attached by a suction cup. If Springer became stranded or separated from her family, the signal from the tag would help the team find her. After a few weeks, the tag would fall off on its own.

Soon after she was released, Lance got a distress call from people saying their boat was being attacked by an orca. Lance raced over in his boat, and he was surprised to see it was Springer!

Springer was rubbing against the boat, and the panicked boaters didn't know what to do. They couldn't start their engine to get away, but they also didn't want her to tip them over.

Lance told them to use their oars and paddle away while he distracted Springer. As they left, Lance saw her satellite tag bobbing in the water. It must have come off when she rubbed against the hull.

Had Springer approached the boaters to be near people? Or was she trying to get the pesky tag off her back? If that was her plan, it didn't work. When Lance saw the tag in the water, he picked it up and put it right back on her!

Happily, Springer never needed an emergency rescue. The satellite tag fell off later as planned.

Researchers noticed that at first Springer swam near but not with her family. After they went to the rubbing beaches together, that changed.

I wondered if she seemed different to the other orcas at first. The team had rubbed lanolin, a kind of lotion, on her skin to keep it from getting dry. Maybe the scent came off when she went to the rubbing beaches, making her seem normal again.

As summer went on, Springer grew stronger and was able to keep up with her family. She spent as much time with her great-aunt Yakat's pod as with her grandmother Kelsey's. Yakat's pod was bigger and included her granddaughter Sunny, who was about the same age as Springer.

Springer had help from whales outside her pod, too. Researchers often saw her with Nodales and Surge, a sister and brother who had also lost their mother. When Springer headed toward a boat, Nodales seemed to steer her away. And they saw Surge share salmon with her, too!

In September, Springer and her family left Johnstone Strait and headed west. Like other resident orcas, they would spend the winter on the central coast of British Columbia, where they were unlikely to be seen.

Springer's rescue had been a success so far. But it wouldn't be considered a complete success until she came back with her family the next year. Over the long winter, all we could do was hope … and wait.

Reunions

July 2003

The next summer, there were two big questions on everyone's mind: Would Springer's family come back to Johnstone Strait? And if they did, would she be with them?

On July 12, Captain Bill Mackay heard that a large group of orcas had entered the strait. He headed west on his whale-watching boat. It was Yakat's pod! And with them was the orca that everyone was waiting to see.

Springer was with her family! They'd returned almost exactly a year after she had come home. The happy news spread up and down the coast, and we all breathed a sigh of relief.

Lance and other researchers got a good look at Springer over the summer. Her skin was clearing up and her saddle patch was easier to see. She was still smaller than other whales her age but otherwise appeared to be a normal, healthy orca.

No matter what happened next, Springer and her family had shown that orcas can go home again and be accepted back into their pods — the first time in history this had ever happened.

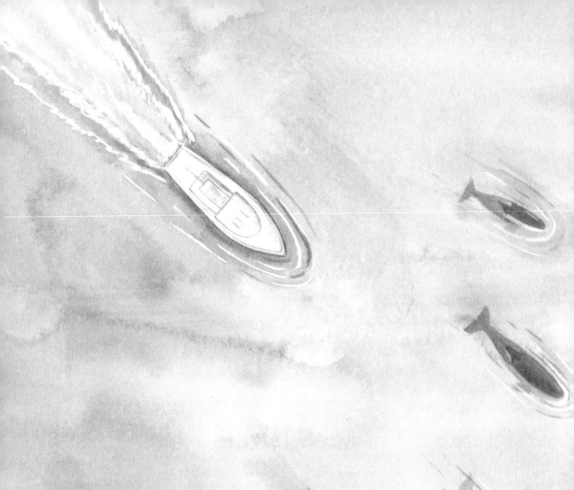

September 2004

It was the same good news
when Springer and her family
returned the next year. Peggy
and I made a quick trip north to see
them. We went whale-watching with
Jim Borrowman aboard his boat, the *Gikumi*.
Almost as soon as we entered Johnstone Strait,
we saw dorsal fins and blows in every direction.
There were orcas everywhere!

Captain Jim kept heading east and then slowed down. "You might want to look over there," he said, pointing toward the Cracroft shore.

Peggy and I looked where he was pointing. We saw a large group of orcas heading west. There were two small dorsal fins on the outside of the group. We looked at each other, then back at the whales. Our hearts raced.

The two little orcas left the group and started swimming toward us. It was Springer and her cousin Sunny! They were heading for the stern of the boat, where Peggy and I were standing. We could barely breathe.

Sunny surfaced first. Then Springer came up, a few yards from the boat. She turned on her side, as if to be sure we saw her saddle patch. For a second, just a second, she looked us in the eyes.

The only way we could have been happier is if the whole team had been there, too. Most of the U.S. team hadn't seen Springer since her journey north. The next day, we started planning a reunion.

July 2007

The Killer Whale Café was buzzing. As each new person came through the door, we cheered. Springer's team was gathered at Telegraph Cove with our families and friends. It was the first time everyone was together since Springer had gone home. Maybe this was what it felt like to be in a superpod!

Captain Jim told us that Springer and her family had returned to the area the day before. They were last seen at the far eastern end of Johnstone Strait. It was hard to sleep that night.

The next day, we boarded the *Gikumi*. Everyone was bundled up. A low-hanging fog had settled on the strait.

We were barely outside Telegraph Cove when we saw one pod, then another and another. Captain Jim kept heading east, slowing down just before we got to Robson Bight. We weren't sure why he'd slowed down until we saw blows, close to shore and heading our way. Yakat's family was approaching.

Suddenly, there they were! Springer surfaced with her cousin Skeena, a young male. A hush fell over the boat as we listened to their blows.

As the orcas crossed Johnstone Strait, we followed slowly behind. There were no other boats or whales around. It was just us as we followed Springer and her family into Blackfish Sound. Ribbons of fog draped the trees.

We passed OrcaLab, where Paul and Helena were watching. The whales kept going until they — and we — were at the entrance to Dong Chong Bay. Five years to the day and almost to the hour, we were with Springer and her family at the place where she'd been released.

We lingered awhile longer. Then we said goodbye to Springer and headed back to Telegraph Cove. We had done our part to bring everyone together. The whales had done the rest.

Springer's Gifts

Over the next decade, Springer grew up. Each summer, we waited to hear if she and her family had returned to Johnstone Strait. In the spring, research teams looked for her during wildlife surveys on the British Columbia coast. Year after year, the news was good. Springer was healthy and growing. Most of the time, she was with Yakat's pod.

Researchers from DFO and the Vancouver Aquarium shared pictures with us. We passed them around like proud aunts and uncles: *Look how big she's getting!* we'd say. *Her saddle patch is so clear!* In 2011, a DFO researcher shared amazing photos of her spyhopping and porpoising. It was hard to believe this healthy, powerful, fully grown orca was the same little whale we remembered.

In 2013, we heard the most exciting news of all: Springer had been seen with her first calf! After the calf survived her first year, the Vancouver Aquarium held a contest to name her. Springer's first calf is called Spirit.

In 2017, we met again in Telegraph Cove to celebrate the 15th anniversary of Springer's return. Just before the reunion, we learned that Springer had been spotted with another calf, who was later named Storm. Springer now has a growing pod of her own.

Springer's return is the first — and so far only — successful orca reunion in history. What did we learn, and what changed, because of Springer, and how can that help orcas today?

Orcas can go home. Before Springer, no one knew if an orca could rejoin its pod. Springer had been away from her family for more than a year, but her pod recognized and accepted her when she returned. This was a scientific first!

People can change and learn from their mistakes.
In the 1960s and 1970s, people were legally capturing
orcas in Washington and British Columbia. Calves were
separated from their mothers and sent to aquariums,
where most of them died within a few years. Thirty years
later, two countries and hundreds of people worked together
to return a single orca to her pod. Springer's return shows
how much we learned about orcas during that time — how
long they live, how far they travel and, most of all, how
important their families are.

How to work together. Getting Springer home was
like a relay race in which everyone played a part. No
one had ever successfully reunited an orca with its pod.
For Springer's sake, we were all willing to try. Over time
and under pressure, the bonds of trust and friendship
between us grew. They connect us still today.

Springer's success showed us what is possible. Today, there are different problems to solve. The southern resident orcas (J, K and L pods) are endangered and could become extinct in fewer than 100 years.

The problems they face are all human-caused. Their favorite food, Chinook salmon, is getting harder and harder to find. The ocean is full of pollution that makes it easier for them to get sick. Boat noise and disturbance make it harder for them to **forage** and hear each other. Together, these threats have made it hard for the orcas to survive.

It's not too late to save the southern residents — yet. Saving an entire population of orcas is harder, and will take longer, than rescuing a single whale. But Springer showed us that when we work together and put the whales first, anything is possible.

In 2008, I founded The Whale Trail, with other members of Springer's team. The Whale Trail is a series of places to watch whales from shore. Today, you can follow the Whale Trail from California to British Columbia, from Seattle to Telegraph Cove.

In the summer of 2020, Springer and her calves returned to Johnstone Strait. She took them to the rubbing beaches, just as her family had taken her. They swam across the smooth stones, rubbing their bellies and backs and sides.

Almost 40 years ago, Springer's great-grandmother was killed near these same beaches. How much has changed!

Springer and her calves are living proof that for as much as people have gotten wrong, we can also get it right. Each of us can make a difference, if we have the courage to try. Like orcas in a pod, we are stronger and more successful when we work together. And most of all, nature can heal, so long as we give it a chance.

The first part of Springer's story has been told. What does her future hold? Will there be enough salmon? Will her family be safe from oil spills, collisions and noise? Like all whales and dolphins, Springer and her family face an uncertain future in rapidly changing seas. What happens next is up to all of us.

Springer in Photos

Marilyn Dahlheim, NOAA Fisheries

Marilyn Dahlheim, NOAA Fisheries

The last known photos of Springer with her mother, Sutlej.

Mark Sears

Springer alone in Puget Sound, 2002.

Lynne Barre, NOAA Fisheries

Springer is lowered onto a barge during her rescue.

Close-up of Springer in Puget Sound. Her skin had a rusty-colored tinge.

Mark Sears

Springer porpoising, 2011.

Springer spyhopping, 2011.

Springer and Spirit, 2019.

Springer near Alert Bay, summer 2020.

Matrilines

Orca **matriline** diagrams show every individual in a family and how they are related, just like human family trees. Vertical lines are drawn between mothers and their calves, and horizontal lines show brothers and sisters.

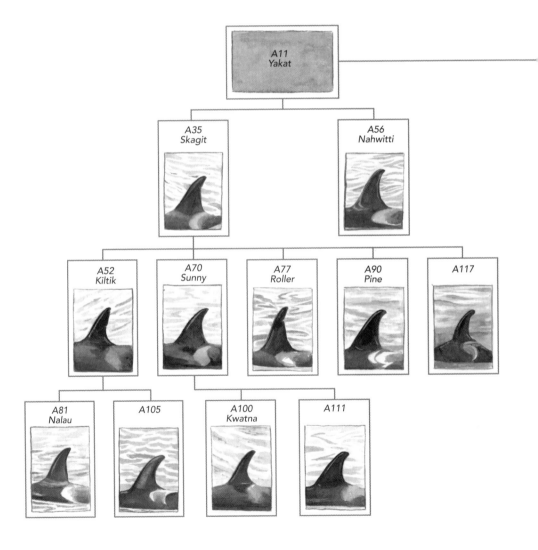

Information source: Towers, Jared, et al. Photo-identification Catalogue and Status of the Northern Resident Killer Whale Population in 2019. Fisheries and Oceans Canada, 2020.

This diagram shows Springer's matriline going back to her great-grandmother A10.

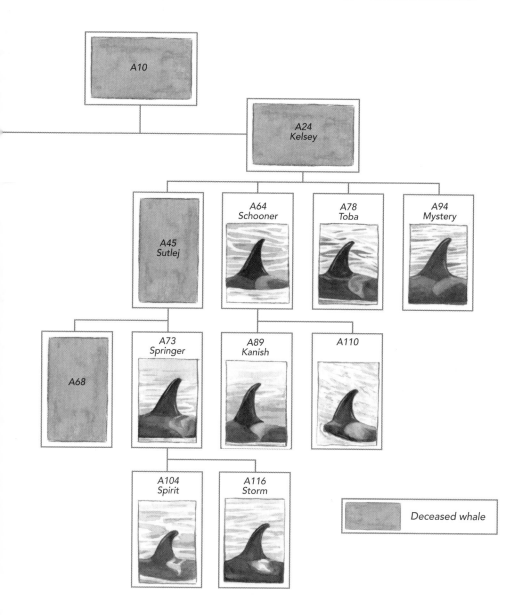

A10

A24
Kelsey

A45
Sutlej

A64
Schooner

A78
Toba

A94
Mystery

A68

A73
Springer

A89
Kanish

A110

A104
Spirit

A116
Storm

Deceased whale

Threats to Whales and Dolphins

Whales and dolphins around the world are threatened by human-caused problems. Old threats such as whaling have never gone away, and new threats are always emerging.

Whaling

Many whale species were hunted for their oil, blubber and meat. In 1986, a global ban on commercial whaling was put in place. Some species, like gray whales, recovered, but others, like right whales, have not. Commercial whaling is still practiced in Norway, Japan and Iceland.

Ship Strikes

When a ship runs into a whale, the collision is usually fatal. Ship strikes are especially a problem for fin whales and blue whales. The large mammals travel through busy shipping lanes and can be hard to see when they rest at the surface.

Entanglements

When whales or dolphins get tangled in nets or other fishing gear, they usually drown. More whales and dolphins die from entanglements than from any other cause.

Captures

The harmful impacts of keeping whales and dolphins in captivity are becoming more well-known. Some countries, including Canada, have banned their capture and display. But others are just getting started.

Noise and Disturbance

Blue whales could once hear one another across the ocean. Today, background noise masks their calls. Sonar exercises, oil drilling and explosions can damage whales' hearing and even kill them. Whale-watching boats can be a problem if there are too many or they come too close.

Climate Change

Ocean warming affects whales, dolphins and their prey. When the ocean heats up, even by a few degrees, it can lead to a decline in fish like salmon, or krill — tiny shrimplike animals that are a source of food for many whales.

Pollution

Toxic chemicals enter marine ecosystems through storm drains, rivers, air and rain. These **toxins** make it easier for whales to get sick. The seas are filled with microplastics — tiny particles that come from plastic products.

There are 89 species of whales and dolphins. Nine are endangered or critically endangered, which means that they need special protection or they will go extinct. In North America, North Atlantic right whales, North Pacific right whales, blue whales, sei whales, southern resident orcas and some populations of beluga whales are endangered.

How You Can Help

The biggest lesson we learned from Springer is that each of us can make a difference. A ferry worker noticed a lone orca and called Mark. A boy spoke up at a crowded public meeting. And paddlers sang when Springer came home. Here are some things you can do to help protect whales, dolphins and their ocean home.

Protect the environment
- Avoid using single-use plastics, such as grocery bags, straws and water bottles.
- Use organic products in your home, garden and school.
- Start or join a recycling program at your school.

Get involved
- Learn more about issues that affect whales and dolphins and support the organizations that are working to protect them.
- Contact an organization to learn how you can help.

Step up and speak out
- Write a letter to a newspaper or local government representative about an environmental issue that matters to you.

Learn More

Books

Ford, John. *Marine Mammals of British Columbia*. Victoria,
    British Columbia: Royal BC Museum, 2017.

Hoyt, Erich. *Encyclopedia of Whales and Dolphins*. Richmond Hill,
    Ontario, and Buffalo, New York: Firefly Books, 2017.

Hoyt, Erich. *Orca: The Whale Called Killer*. Revised ed. Richmond
    Hill, Ontario, and Buffalo, New York: Firefly Books, 2019.

Valice, Kim Perez. *The Orca Scientists*. New York: HMH Books
    for Young Readers, 2018.

Vickers, Roy Henry, and Robert Budd. *Orca Chief*. Madeira Park,
    British Columbia: Harbour Publishing, 2015.

Organizations and Websites

The Whale Trail: www.thewhaletrail.org

Seattle Aquarium: www.seattleaquarium.org

Whale Museum: www.whalemuseum.org

The Whale Interpretive Centre: www.killerwhalecentre.org

American Cetacean Society: www.acsonline.org

BC Cetacean Sighting Network: www.wildwhales.org

NOAA: www.noaa.gov

DFO: www.dfo-mpo.gc.ca

Raincoast Conservation: www.raincoast.org

Georgia Strait Alliance: www.georgiastrait.org

Far East Russia Orca Project: www.russianorca.com

Glossary

blow: a spout of water sprayed by a whale surfacing to breathe

blowhole: a whale's nostril, located at the top of its head

catamaran: a boat with two hulls

cetaceans: a group of marine mammals that includes whales, dolphins and porpoises

Department of Fisheries and Oceans (DFO): now called Fisheries and Oceans Canada, the government agency in Canada that studies and manages Canada's oceans and freshwater areas

dorsal fin: the fin rising from the back of most whales, dolphins and porpoises

echolocation: the use of sounds (sometimes described as clicks) and echoes that allow orcas to determine the direction and distance of objects in the water, including prey

ecotype: a distinct population of a species that is especially adapted to a particular set of environmental conditions. The three ecotypes of orcas in the Pacific Northwest are resident orcas, Bigg's or transient orcas and offshore orcas.

fecal sample: a small amount of an animal's feces (poop) collected to help understand more about the animal's diet and health

First Nations: a term that describes the original inhabitants of Canada, in addition to Inuit. The term "Native Americans" is used in the United States.

forage: to search and hunt for food

hydrophone: an underwater microphone used to hear sounds in water

ketosis: the process of breaking down fat (blubber) for energy

killer whale: another name for orca

matriarch: the oldest female whale in a pod or family group

matriline: a family unit organized around the mother, including all of her offspring (sons and daughters) and the offspring of all the females in this family. The matriline can range from one to four generations.

National Oceanic and Atmospheric Administration (NOAA): a U.S. government agency that conducts research on the world's oceans and atmosphere and conserves and manages coastal and marine ecosystems

Native American: a term that describes the original inhabitants of the United States. The term "First Nations" is used in Canada, along with Inuit.

net pen: an enclosure in an open area of water, created out of nets

Orphan Orca Fund: a group of seven nonprofit organizations in the Seattle, Washington area that worked together to support Springer. The organizations were: People for Puget Sound, the American Cetacean Society — Puget Sound Chapter, Orca Alliance, The Whale Museum, Orca Conservancy, Friends of the San Juans and Earth Island Institute.

pectoral fins: the flippers on the underside of a whale, behind its head, used mainly for balance and steering

pod: a group of whales that usually includes an extended family (or more than one matriline) of orca mothers and their offspring

rostrum: the very front end of a whale's, dolphin's or porpoise's head, also called the beak or snout

saddle patch: the gray area behind an orca's dorsal fin. Saddle patches are unique to each whale and can be used to identify individual animals.

tail flukes: the two flattened fins that make up a whale's tail, larger on male orcas than females

toxin: a poisonous substance, such as a pesticide

Springer's Team

Springer's team was led by NOAA Fisheries, DFO and the Vancouver Aquarium, with strong support from the community. The Orphan Orca Fund was a group of seven nonprofit organizations that worked together to support NOAA. Independent researchers in Canada and the United States volunteered hundreds of hours of time to monitor Springer. Businesses contributed supplies for Springer's rescue, rehabilitation, transport and release.

NOAA Fisheries

Bob Lohn
Joe Scordino
Brent Norberg
Brad Hanson
Lynne Barre
Amy Sloan
Janet Whaley
Carrie Hubard
Brian Gorman
Janet Sears

Other members of NOAA Team

Pete Schroeder, DVM
Jeff Foster
Stephen Claussen
Jim Horton
Brian O'Neill
Peter Noah
Jen Schorr
Greg Schorr
Steve Sinelli
Stephen Raverty, DVM
Jim McBain, DVM

Washington Department of Fish and Wildlife

Steve Jeffries
Dyanna Lambourn

DFO

John Ford
Graeme Ellis
Marilyn Joyce
Lara Sloan
Jared Towers

Orphan Orca Fund

Kathy Fletcher
Donna Sandstrom
Peggy Foreman
Uko Gorter
Joe Olson
Ann Stateler
Odin Lonning
Sally Hodson
Will Anderson
Kristine Stebbins
Dave Bain
Fred Felleman
Michael Harris
Kelley Balcomb-Bartok
Stephanie Buffum

OrcaLab

Paul Spong
Helena Symonds

Vancouver Aquarium (now an Ocean Wise initiative)

John Nightingale
Clint Wright
Lance Barrett-Lennard
Dave Huff, DVM
Caitlin Birdsall

Field Research and Other Help

Mark Sears
Jim and Mary Borrowman
Bill and Donna Mackay
Bob McLaughlin
Bob Wood
Matt Nichols
Mike Bennett

Businesses That Helped

Cypress Island Inc.
The Friendly Foam Shop
Home Depot
Manson Construction
Nichols Brothers Boat Builders
Point Defiance Zoo & Aquarium
SeaWorld
Six Flags Marine World
Underwater Sports
Woodland Park Zoo
And more!

Author's Note

When I got back to Seattle after watching Springer go home, I had dinner with a friend. I was still so excited that the story tumbled out as fast as I could tell it. When I was done, my friend asked if I would write it down. The seed for this book was planted that night.

I wrote this book to tell the story of Springer's return, and to honor the people who made it happen. Many of these stories haven't been told before, and would have been lost to time. I also wanted to inspire young readers. I hope this book encourages you to find what you love to do, and use your talents to make the world a better place. Never doubt that you can make a difference.

It takes a pod to publish a book! Thank you to Kids Can Press, especially editors Yasemin Uçar and Kathleen Keenan, for bringing this story so beautifully to life. And to Sarah Burwash, whose warm illustrations light up every page. The spirit of Springer shines through.

How does a salmon find its way back to the stream where it was born? My journey with the orcas has felt like that — a deep, instinctive pull toward home. Warmest thanks to the friends who kept faith in this story and me, and pointed the way when the path wasn't clear. Especially to Erich Hoyt, whose book, *Orca: The Whale Called Killer*, opened the door to the orcas for me and so many others.

Thanks most of all to Springer, who changed our lives as surely as we changed hers, and who still plays with sticks! And to the orcas, who found me in a dream, and never let me go.

DONNA SANDSTROM has been writing since she was old enough to hold a pencil. She fell in love with orcas when she moved to Seattle from California, where she grew up. In 2002, she participated in Springer's rescue as a citizen organizer. She founded and directs The Whale Trail from her home in West Seattle, where she watches for dorsal fins. This is her first book.

SARAH BURWASH is a visual artist working in a variety of media including watercolor, collage, ceramics, animation, illustration and comics. Her work is both imaginative and rooted in her lived experiences, including cabin building, forest stewarding, motorcycling and crewing on a fishing vessel. Her work has been exhibited in Canada, the United States and Europe. Originally from kEluwi'sst (Rossland), British Columbia, she lives and works in Unama'ki (Cape Breton Island), Nova Scotia.

Alert Bay

Hanson Island

Johnstone Strait

Telegraph
Cove

Campbell River

Vancouver
Island

Pacific Ocean

Strait of Juan de Fuca